FAITH
— *in the* —
INNER CITY

A History of St Alban's School and Academy

FAITH
in the
INNER CITY

A History of St Alban's School and Academy

Peter T. Marsh

BREWIN BOOKS

First published by
Brewin Books Ltd, 56 Alcester Road,
Studley, Warwickshire B80 7LG in 2013
www.brewinbooks.com

© Peter T. Marsh 2013.

All rights reserved.

ISBN: 978-1-85858-503-1

The moral rights of the authors have been asserted.

A Cataloguing in Publication Record
for this title is available from the British Library.

Typeset in Minion Pro
Printed in Great Britain by
T J International Ltd.

CONTENTS

Introduction	vi
1. The Founding Faith	1
2. In the Wake of the Founders	10
3. Dual Challenge: Demolition and the Diocese	19
4. Recovering in Exceptionally Challenging Circumstances	34
5. Extending Faith in the Inner City	42

INTRODUCTION

This is a story of the convergence of two forms of faith in the inner city brought together by the social and religious reconstruction of a neighbourhood that both sought to serve. Highgate has always been one of the poorest wards in England from its initial construction in the middle of the nineteenth century with shoddy back-to-backs on the inner edge of Birmingham through the demolition of that housing in the mid-twentieth century and its replacement with tower blocks and maisonettes. Its destitution at the outset touched the heart of two Irish priests from the Church of England who expressed their faith by building schools and churches to serve the very poor. The community that grew up around church and school was torn apart in the 1960s by the demolition and reconstruction of its housing. The former residents were scattered to the outer edges of the city while migrants from distant corners of the former empire moved in to seek improvement for themselves and their families.

The accompanying transformation of what had been a largely Christian neighbourhood into a largely non-Christian one, still God-fearing but religiously divided, perplexed the governors and trustees of St Alban's school. All were appointed by the Church of England, whether by the parish church or by the Diocese of Birmingham, yet few in the community were adherents of the Church of England. The parish church now drew its congregation from across the city and beyond. The school had nevertheless been founded and generously endowed to uphold the faith that inspired its founders as well as to serve the local community; and commitment to that faith was legally entrenched through the Voluntary Aided Church of England status of the school. The parish church and the diocese struggled for nearly thirty years, usually at odds with each other, to work out a way to deal with this uneasy relationship between church and community; and during that struggle the school came close to closure.

The school found its way forward at the end of the twentieth century by extending the inclusive ethos on which the Church of England had long prided

Right: Thomas Pollock.

itself to encompass the variety of faiths now practised in Highgate. Students at St Alban's were taught to strengthen their own faith while learning to understand and respect the faith of others. But by then the school faced a heightened challenge on another front; and the spectre of closure continued to hang over it. In 1989 the national inspectorate of schools challenged the hitherto common assumption that children in poor communities like Highgate were unlikely to reach high levels of educational attainment. A decade later the New Labour government launched a series of initiatives to help schools in such neighbourhoods; and St Alban's was targeted by two of these programmes. One, which came to be known as the Octet project, focused on the exceptionally challenging circumstances faced by eight schools including St Alban's. Through participation in this project with generous accompanying financial support from the ministry of education, St Alban's markedly improved its performance, but not enough to guarantee its survival.

The second of these initiatives, the one that came to epitomise the policy of New Labour in education, was the academies programme launched by Andrew Adonis who then became Minister for Schools. It aimed to find sponsors for underperforming schools to provide them with independent governance, an endowment and guidance in single-minded pursuit of improvement in teaching and learning. Through this programme, St Alban's found a sponsor known by the acronym ARK whose faith in the inner city complemented the quite different faith of the school's founders. Although ARK stressed its lack of religious affiliation, it insisted in the almost religious accents of a faith in things unseen that children in poor inner-city neighbourhoods could be brought to levels of attainment in education as high as those reached by children in affluent suburbs. The fusion of these two faiths has lifted St Alban's, now an academy, to the national distinction it enjoys today and to the opening of its new building.

This story ranging over 150 years from the 1860s into the twenty-first century could not have been written without the remarkable records stored in the archives of the Central Library in Birmingham, of the National Society in London, and above all in the school governors' minutes preserved by Mary Goodman who helped to save the school as governor, treasurer and trustee over more than half a century.

Left: James Pollock.

Chapter 1

THE FOUNDING FAITH

Birmingham had a growing, painful awareness of the needs of its rapidly expanding population in the 1860s. People kept crowding in, drawn by the prospect of employment in the factories that sprang up all over the town, small ones close to the town centre, large ones on its periphery. But as a young town, Birmingham had few provisions to meet the needs of all these people, few churches or hospitals or schools, and those few were targeted at the wealthy.

This situation haunted a number of wealthy men, most of them born elsewhere, who were themselves drawn to the town – it was not yet a city – by the economic opportunities and social and religious challenges it presented. The call for social action came from ministers of religion, most of them Nonconformists, pre-eminently George Dawson at the Church of the Saviour in the Jewellery Quarter and R.W. Dale at Carr's Lane Congregational chapel in the town centre. The civic gospel that they preached found its greatest practitioner in Joseph Chamberlain, the metal manufacturer who proceeded to turn Birmingham from one of the worst into one of the best governed cities in Britain. The first collective action that these men took was to found the National Education League to press Parliament for legislation requiring local authorities to make sure that there were enough elementary schools to accommodate every child in the country. The Church of England had been trying to do that for more than sixty years through the National Society for the Education of the Poor in the Principles of the Established Church; and for the past thirty years the efforts of the National Society had been supported financially by the state. But by the 1860s it was clear that these efforts had fallen far short of the crying need.

Two clergymen of the Church of England, brothers from Ireland, tackled the problem more directly. James Pollock and his young brother Thomas felt drawn to one of the most deprived corners of Birmingham, a neglected wedge of swampy land along the River Rea called Highgate where polluting workshops and shoddy back-to-back housing were being hastily constructed. The back-to-backs sheltered families in need of work close to where they lived. The first wave of newcomers was soon joined by even poorer families evicted from the sewage laden, disease infested rookeries nearby in the town centre. When Joseph Chamberlain became mayor of the town, he had these slums demolished to make way for a corridor of grand shops and lawyers' offices which he named Corporation Street to honour the town council. Chamberlain's scheme improved the centre greatly but made no provision for the people it dispossessed. Highgate, empty fields until 1830, was turned during the 1860s and '70s into an instant slum.

Its destitution touched the hearts and souls of the Pollock brothers. Father Tom in particular was infuriated by the filth and pollution amid which the jerry-built housing of Highgate was built. 'If I breathe bad air, or live in dirt willingly, I am a suicide,' he cried, 'if I force others to do this, or do not do my best to help them, I am a murderer.' The Pollocks were disciples of the Oxford Movement, a revival of Catholic tradition in the Church of England later called Anglo-Catholicism, which broke with the Protestant treatment of salvation as an individual matter to emphasize the importance of the church. The concern of Anglo-Catholics with the corporate social responsibilities of the church was further enhanced by their renewed stress on the doctrine of the incarnation, of God taking on human form. Hence the care lavished by clergy like the Pollocks on the densely packed concentrations of mankind forced to live in destitution in England's inner urban heart. Clergy with that intensity of social commitment came to be known as Christian Socialists. The Pollocks also sympathised with the Anglo-Catholic attempt through elaborate ceremony, vestments and incense to bring the beauty of holiness into the squalor of the slums. But what distinguished their ministry among the followers of the Oxford Movement was the centrality of children and hence of schools in their sense of mission. They opened their first church in 1865, named St Alban's after the first English martyr, in a building designed to serve temporarily as a school as well as place for worship.

They were therefore ready when Parliament passed the epoch making Education Act of 1870. It gave the Church just one more year to build schools

1. The Founding Faith

wherever the current provision was inadequate. Then, going a long way toward the demands of the National Education League, local school boards would be elected to meet the remaining need. James Pollock immediately applied to the National Society for financial support, but without success. Undaunted, the Pollocks and wealthy supporters from nearby Moseley and Edgbaston raised £2,000 to enlarge their school so that it could accommodate 460 boys, girls and infants and thus remove the need for board schools in Highgate. The whole country threw itself into a frenzy of school building in the early 1870s when the first school boards were elected. No place drew more attention than Birmingham where Chamberlain and his allies from the National Education League commissioned the construction of the towering neo-gothic schools that still mark the skyline of Birmingham. The Pollocks' schools in Highgate were architecturally more modest, but they matched the board schools of Birmingham in scale.

Even so, the Pollocks were hard pressed to keep up with the demand in their parish. The population of Highgate trebled in the first fifteen years of their mission there. Numbering around 4,500 when they opened their first church and school, it doubled in six years and reached nearly 13,000 within another decade. To keep pace, the Pollocks had to build schools at an industrial pace, much more than they could afford. They appealed again to the National Society for a grant and were grateful for the £25 they received. Still the expanding population of Highgate exceeded their efforts, and they had to turn children away from their schools until much expanded accommodation could be built. With the opening in 1880 of a grand new church, the former building was turned into a school with separate establishments for boys, girls and infants to accommodate a staggering total of 1,262 children.

The rapid expansion of St Alban's schools and the popular demand for admission to them were all the more astonishing because the entire experience was new. Everything and everyone was new to the community; and school too was a new experience for almost everyone in Highgate except for the Pollock brothers who had been educated at Trinity College, Dublin. The challenge in Highgate was heightened by the poverty of the people. St Alban's schools were not yet free: the children had to pay 2 pence, raised in 1873 to 3 pence per week to attend the schools and were sent home if they were a penny short. The schools, like the back-to-back houses beside them, had little heat, and many children came in winter as in summer without shoes. The discipline of schooling, there by 8:15 with just three weeks off in midsummer, was a harsh change for street urchins. Fevers that turned readily into epidemics kept children from school and killed pupils and teachers alike. And the teaching was patchy, heavily reliant on pupil teachers who struggled to obtain the required qualifications as they taught. Much depended on the head teacher, whose health was prone to buckle under the strain. But the Pollock brothers were there daily. Father James sometimes taught arithmetic as well as Scripture, and while he soon settled into a pattern of weekly attendance, Father Tom continued daily. The schools were his dearest care.

The relationship between St Alban's schools and the Birmingham School Board was unavoidably tense because the Board was both competitor and regulator. Its first concern was to establish board schools with minimal religious education wherever the supply of church schools was inadequate; and strict secularists like Joseph Chamberlain made no secret of their aim to replace the church schools entirely. The School Board was also required to enforce the requirements that the education ministry in London laid down for all schools, whether religious or secular, in receipt of its financial support on which they all depended. Her Majesty's Inspectors (HMIs) were sent in to monitor attainment in secular subjects, and the education ministry also set standards for school buildings, the ratio of staff to students, class size and student attendance. While the Pollocks guarded the religious autonomy of their schools jealously and could boast that all their schools were constructed without public money, they worked cooperatively with the local authority in the early years, particularly on matters of common concern such as truancy. They accepted the need for governmental as well as diocesan inspection and strove to ensure that their teachers held government certification. They were 'determined not only to maintain, but also to improve, the high reputation which St Alban's Schools have gained among Elementary Schools in Birmingham.' By 1877 board schools were up and running all over the town, and they attracted some children in Highgate away from the church schools, though there was more than enough demand to keep all the schools full. The problem in fact for St Alban's was to hold down the size of its classes to comply with governmental requirements.

Father Tom and a class at the girls' school in the 1880s, photograph reproduced with the permission of Birmingham Libraries & Archives, MS1285/2/124.

Then as now, everyone was struck by the low level of literacy among the children of Highgate. The first entry in the log book of the girls' school noted, 'Children very backward indeed in everything.' At admission few children could read at all. These low levels of literacy made the achievement at St Alban's schools in their first decade all the more remarkable. The teaching staff remained small: at the girls' school it consisted of the headmistress, one certified assistant, four pupil teachers and a candidate pupil teacher as well as contributions from the clergy. A new headmistress took over in the mid-1870s and immediately tightened up on attendance, punctuality, discipline, home work and the performance of the students especially in mathematics. In 1880 the HMI inspecting the girls' school judged that the reading, writing and arithmetic there were 'good'. (No log books have survived for the boys' school.)

However, the challenge to St Alban's schools mounted inexorably higher. They were heavily dependent on funding from the education ministry at

Westminster, and it used its financial power to raise standards by coupling its grants with assessment of student performance. HMI inspections took place annually and grew ever more detailed and exacting. The inspector of the girls' school in 1883, for example, judged 'Reading and Dictation good. Arithmetic very weak in the fourth standard. The first standard had not a proper knowledge of Tables. Sewing well taught. It is only with the greatest possible hesitation that I feel justified in recommending the Grant for Geography.' Though St Alban's schools struggled to keep pace with the rising standards, Father Tom could boast in 1891 that they were the largest and among the best in the whole diocese of Worcester of which Birmingham then formed part.

But his mood was simultaneously darkened at the national level by the abolition of fees for attendance at board schools. Joseph Chamberlain extracted this concession, long a cardinal objective of the National Education League, from a Conservative government that depended on support from his Liberal Unionists. Though the concession was financially costly for the government, it was impossible to resist on social grounds. Implicitly, however, it placed church schools in danger. Because state funding could not go directly to religious organisations, church schools would have to go on charging fees, losing students to the now free board schools, and in many cases would wither away. This was precisely what secularists like Joseph Chamberlain and Nonconformist opponents of the Church of England like R.W. Dale had always wanted.

Father Tom issued a cry of alarm. He saw how free education at board schools and the soaring standards demanded by the education ministry to qualify for government grants could combine to drive church schools to the wall. He knew full well how ignorance bred disease, destitution and unemployment on the streets of Highgate. But that understanding only intensified his plea for total care of children, their souls as well as their minds and bodies, which only church schools could provide. Without religious underpinning, schools were in his estimation essentially heathen institutions. Speaking to the Junior Clergy Club of Birmingham, Father Tom argued that 'Nothing can be a substitute for the steady systematic instruction in religious truth and duty by trained teachers. Nothing can make up for the loss of the bond which the teaching and learning of religious truth and duty create between teachers and children, and the hallowing of all the school work by the prayers … a child is a sacred thing. No one is fit to be trusted with children – with the forming of their minds and characters, who does not feel an awe over him in his work, who does not reverence the children as those whom Christ gathers in His arms even now.' He pursued his argument in biting verse:

> 'Our city in its wisdom has decided
> That man's short life in two may be divided;
> No child to learn his grammar may refuse,
> About religion he is free to choose.
> Make sharp his wits, and, as they do in France,
> Leave his religion to be learned by chance.
> Trust conscience, true or blinded, weak or strong,
> To tell him what is right and what is wrong.
> Eternal things perhaps may be of worth;
> The one thing needful is to thrive on Earth.
> No teacher may refer to One on High,
> To fix the standard of morality.
>   Shame on us if S. Alban's Schools reveal
> The lack of earnest self-denying zeal,
> No larger Schools the Diocese can show,
> Nor any better, we rejoice to know.
> They have a work to do, to guide our youth
> In ways of highest wisdom, fullest truth;
> To train the nature, not a part of it
> To quicken conscience, and not only wit.'

To counter the threat from free education at board schools, Father Tom called still in verse upon wealthy high churchmen in nearby Moseley and Edgbaston to support:

> 'Our schools – no cause comes closer to the heart,
> Of all our works the proudest hardest part.
> You love S. Alban's – help S. Alban's Schools;
> So test your zeal, obey the first of rules,
> The lambs must be the Shepherd's dearest care.'

By 1894, with England in the throes of another recession, he was desperate, and he pleaded once again for support from the National Society. 'The Parish is very poor, and grows poorer from the gradual migration towards the further suburbs. ... The schools are full, and had we twice the accommodation, I believe that every place would be taken. ... The wealthy friends who helped in the early years of our work, have either died or left the neighbourhood.' There were now two large board schools in the parish and another on its borders, and the Pollocks were determined to keep pace with them in efficiency. The most recent HMI inspection bore out Father Tom's claims about the performance of the boys' school but more hesitantly of the girls'. The HMI inspection also called for an immediate strengthening of the staff at the boys' school and improved accommodation at all three schools, boys', girls' and infants'. New building standards set by the government required a refitting of two cloak rooms, rebuilding of the girls' school offices, and reconstruction of the boys' school offices to provide better sanitation, at a total cost of £250.

The National Society examined the financial position of St Alban's schools closely. Of their total annual income of just over £2000, a little over £360 came from fees. Local voluntary donations, church collections and money from bazaars raised another £380. The grants from the education ministry at Westminster amounted to £575. That sum was exceeded by a bank overdraft of £650 for which the Pollocks had assumed personal responsibility. The National Society agreed to a grant of £25.

Encouraged by this meagre award, the Pollocks and their fellow school managers managed to increase the size of the teaching staff and see to their improvement in qualification. The HMI inspector the next year 'expressed himself satisfied with the working of the school ... Each of his suggestions have as far as possible been carried out; with a decided improvement to the work of the school.' Again the following year the HMI testified that 'The discipline and tone in this school are all that can be desired, and some of the teaching is very satisfactory.' There was still plenty of room for improvement: in reading, 'there is a want of intelligent expressions and good articulation ... Grammar and Mental Arithmetic should be less mechanical.' He concluded, 'I shall look for a general improvement in the quality of the teaching as a condition of the continued recommendation of the higher grant though I fully recognise the industry of all

1. The Founding Faith

the Teachers.' The diocesan inspector was more effusive and awarded the school 'a high position in the A Class.'

But the year ended as it had begun on a sombre note. The school had opened the previous January 'under very painful circumstances' with the news that Father James had died just before Christmas. Less than a year later, the log book of the girls' school recorded, 'Words cannot express the sorrow that has been felt in this school this week. Death has removed the much loved and respected Manager the Revd. T.B. Pollock. ... For 30 years the two Mr. Pollocks have worked giving their time and substance for the benefit of the poor of this district.' It was the end of an era. With the death of the Pollock brothers, the schools' grasp of the vision of their founders also weakened.

Chapter 2

IN THE WAKE OF THE FOUNDERS

'I am sorry to write … "bad" in a Report of one of St. Alban's Schools,' the diocesan inspector observed within a year of Father Tom's death, '& I cannot understand what can have led to so sad a downfall.' It is easy in historical retrospect to account for this precipitate downfall. The magnitude and quality of St Alban's Schools reflected the belief of the Pollock brothers, rare even among disciples of the Oxford Movement, that their schools were every bit as important as the churches they built. They designed the first structures that they built to serve as both church and school. They looked after their schools as closely as they tended to the pastoral needs of their parish. In addition to daily supervision, they served as managers of their schools, and they exhausted their personal wealth to build them up. When Father Tom died, it was discovered that he had personally guaranteed the thousand pound overdraft upon which the schools depended. With his death, St Alban's Schools lost inspiration, governance and a dependable financial base.

The parish of St Alban's was an appreciative beneficiary of the Pollocks' mission in education, and the wealthy members of the congregation contributed to it financially, but that was all. The diocese of Worcester to which Birmingham belonged provided no more than encouraging inspections. The financial support provided by the National Society as the agency of the Church of England in education was meagre. As for the Birmingham school board and the education ministry in London, both of them heavily influenced by the National Education League, they were more suspicious than supportive of St Alban's as the largest set of church schools in the city, as Birmingham had now become. Without the ceaseless dedication of the Pollocks, St Alban's Schools would not have flourished as they did. More than half a century would pass before vicars of St Alban's would again treat the school as of crucial importance to church and parish.

2. In the Wake of the Founders

Though stunned by the loss within a year of both brothers, the parish church took matters in hand with the appointment of new church wardens, Arthur Dixon and John Goodman. The vicars of St Alban's now concerned themselves primarily with the church, devolving much of the responsibility for management of the schools upon these laymen. Dixon and Goodman threw themselves into the work as ardent Anglo-Catholics, a commitment intensified by the appeal of the poverty of Highgate to Dixon as a Christian socialist. Even so, as working architects they could not provide day-to-day supervision as the Pollocks had done; and the structure of the school management was overhauled accordingly. The task that confronted the wardens as school managers was daunting. They faced a rapid turnover in the demoralised teaching staff and a decline in their number, which greatly increased the burden on the head teachers and undermined discipline among the children. Both the performance of the schools and their financial position deteriorated. The schools lacked funding to bring the staff back up to strength. 'We are dreadfully in debt,' one of the clergy wrote to the National Society, '– this year £100 worse than last year.' Dixon, with fewer architectural commissions than Goodman, undertook to check on children whose attendance was irregular while Goodman concentrated on the building demands emanating from London. The education ministry ruled that the infants' school was not large enough to accommodate its current enrolment satisfactorily and ordered an enlargement.

The demands of the ministry increased with passage of another major Education Act in 1902. The infants' school had to be completely demolished and two adjoining cottages purchased to make room along the densely packed streets of Highgate for a two-storey building for a girls' and infants' school to accommodate 350 instead of the current 170. And the number of girls and infants at St Alban's continued to expand, though the number of boys fell as they took advantage of new board schools close at hand. Walking quietly in Father Tom's footsteps, John Goodman bore much of the cost of all this expansion privately without adding to the schools' debt. Funding was also found to build up the teaching staff.

The performance of the schools did not improve immediately. The HMI in 1903 still stressed 'a falling away from a high standard in some of the work.' By the following year, however, the inspector praised the managers for paying attention to his recommendations. He acknowledged that the staff was now competent and 'the work generally ... in an improving state.' By 1911 the inspector of the boys' school pointed out that though it was 'situated in a poor neighbourhood ... [the] results ... are far above average, and demonstrate the wisdom of furnishing the School with a strong Staff.' The school still suffered from its cramped site with little room for games and exercise outdoors. 'But the final product as seen in the two higher classes, and especially in the highest, is highly creditable to all concerned. The outstanding features of the School are the unusual alertness and intelligence of the first class, the intelligence and interest shown in using books, the fluency and relevancy of the oral composition, the willing co-operation between teachers and boys, and the amiable bearing of the latter.' The inspector from the newly created diocese of Birmingham was even more impressed: 'The work here,' he reported, 'the influences exerted and the whole general tone strike one as ideal.'

The expanded girls' school was no longer overcrowded. But in 1913 the Board of Education in London decreed that unless similar improvements were made to the boys' school, it would lose its accreditation. Accordingly when war broke out in Europe, St Alban's found itself again engaged in a building campaign, this time to replace the original dual-use church and school building that the Pollocks had erected. The new building would accommodate twice the number in the girls' school; but because the war increased the difficulty of fund raising, John Goodman designed a building for the boys that reduced the cost of expansion in overcrowded Highgate by turning the roof of the school into its playground. The new building was opened in 1915 during the 50th anniversary celebration of the founding of St Alban's church and school.

The HMI report on the girls' school next year was guarded. Its size was once again a matter of concern, with six classes crowded into two rooms. Still more serious was the amount of staff illness. The teacher of the first class and the chief assistant teacher were away for much of the year, increasing the demands on the head mistress who was already often absent through illness; and governmental regulation prevented the managers from appointing temporary replacements. Illness kept the head teacher away for lengthening periods as the war dragged to

Right: The boys' school built in 1915 on Leopold Street, photograph courtesy of John Pomphrett.

its close, and the school generally deteriorated. The building suffered from inattention. An inspection in the autumn of 1918 noted that 'sweeping and cleaning have been very unsatisfactorily done of late. The windows are so dirty that on a dull afternoon it is impossible to see to work properly … Neither the children's nor the teachers' lavatories were washed out during the weekend and the former have been in a filthy condition all the week. … In a school like this it is necessary that children should be taught cleanliness, but the lessons must be wasted when illustrated in a dirty school.' Had the vicar looked in on the school daily as Father Tom had done, this rebuke would not have occurred.

Wartime regulation of employment kept the schools short of staff until 1919. Over the following two years, however, the performance of the girls' school was raised to pre-war levels. Once again the school was clean, and the children were better behaved, reflecting better teaching. The curriculum was enriched, particularly in history to broaden 'the children's outlook and sympathies through lessons on the civilisation of the past' – but the instruction still suffered from the lack of text-books. Arithmetic was the weakest subject. And the school was again overcrowded. But the main problem at the girls' school was the continuing,

eventually prolonged illness of the head mistress reluctant to retire. The appointment at last in 1925 of a new head teacher transformed the situation. Text books, maps and dictionaries flowed in, the teaching was reorganised and fresh syllabi drawn up. The HMI report for 1928 reported that 'Systematic work has been done to strengthen the foundations of Arithmetic & the backward children are receiving special attention. ... There is also definite improvement in the oral English of the upper classes. ... In Standard VI & Standard V, where specialist teaching has been introduced, the children are showing a lively interest in their work which they discuss freely under stimulating instruction. Written English, however, is not yet free from elementary errors.'

The outlook for St Alban's schools was profoundly changed in the early 1930s by a range of governmental initiatives. Since the death of the Pollocks, the fortunes of the threefold school – boys', girls' and infants' – had followed an up-and-down pattern of deterioration and improvement interspersed with bouts of expansion. Children moved up year by year from the infants' school through the boys' or girls' schools to departure at age 14. The girls commonly then went into service in shops or the affluent homes of nearby Moseley while the boys sought employment in the workshops and small factories within walking distance of home. This familiar pattern was shaken up by movement at the national level towards raising the school leaving age to 15. This movement took place only gradually and would not be completed until well after the Second World War. But from the outset it had institutional consequences because it was accompanied by a similarly gradual separation of primary from secondary education for the upper years from age 11. And this separation involved another gradual reorganisation throughout the country of all governmentally funded schooling including that of the Church of England.

There was general agreement that St Alban's would emerge from this reorganisation as a senior or secondary school, though it was reluctant to lose its junior side completely. Dudley Clark as vicar explained to his congregation before the war that 'S. Alban's school holds a very high place in the estimation of the local education authority ... our scholastic and athletic successes during the last few years have been an object of admiration and envy.' St Alban's boys had distinguished themselves on the cricket field while individual girls as well as boys from St Alban's won entrance scholarships to the city's grammar schools.

2. In the Wake of the Founders

No one thought that St Alban's school might one day educate its inner-city students all the way to university entrance. The conversion of St Alban's into a secondary school involved immediate preparatory costs of £1000 to reduce the size of classes to no more than 40. When the changes were completed, 430 students were to be placed on its books, an enrolment that St Alban's would not substantially exceed for the following seventy years.

Significant though raising the national school leaving age to 15 was for St Alban's, the change that Birmingham made in its policy for housing had an even greater impact on the school. Highgate had been built quickly and cheaply in the nineteenth century out of the notorious back-to-backs, densely packed housing that bred disease and destitution. The slum clearance schemes to which Birmingham periodically resorted only made matters worse by failing to provide affordable housing for the dispossessed. Daunted by the cost of any thoroughgoing solution, the city pursued a delaying policy of repairs and improvements to the rickety structures. At last in 1930 city officials faced up to the necessity of replacing back-to-backs in the poorest city-centre wards; and they started with Highgate. The council designated a five-acre site in the heart of Highgate to be bounded by Angelina, Dymoke, Leopold and Vaughton Streets. There an experimental block of flats was to be constructed, named by the road that crossed the site as the Emily Street Slum Clearance Scheme.

Dudley Clark was uneasy about the implications of the scheme: 'it seems quite likely,' he wrote in the parish magazine, 'that we shall in time cease to be a residential district. If the authorities could give us some idea as to whether many of the houses in the parish are likely to be condemned as unfit for human habitation and whether such houses are likely to be replaced by other houses or factories, it would be easier to decide whether it is really necessary to enlarge the present [school] buildings.' He remained uneasy even when the details of the scheme were more clearly laid out: 'While the departure of the old houses will not be regretted by anybody, we shall be sorry to lose from our midst those who have lived there for a long time, but we can hardly grudge them the new homes that will be provided for them even though they may be some distance away.'

Highgate would never be the same. The homes of more than 1,200 people were to be torn down, and while some of the residents would be re-housed in vacant slum buildings elsewhere in the city centre, others were to be despatched to the outer fringes of the city, far from the friends and institutions amid which they had grown up. No matter how economically deprived, indeed because of their destitution, the people of Highgate had turned themselves into a tightly knit, mutually dependent community. Church and school were central to that community. But now many of its members were to be torn away, most of them never to return. Some would make their way back to the church on Sundays, drawn by the majestic beauty of its liturgy and services. But the children who left Highgate would have to enrol in other schools, leaving St Alban's with empty seats that threatened its survival. Enrolment at the school fell with every hammer blow at the surrounding housing while the noise of the wreckers drowned out the teachers. Rubbing in the loss after two years of demolition, the Local Education Authority told the senior school to reduce its teaching staff in line with the fall in student numbers.

The outbreak of World War II effectively suspended the institutional changes to the school. During the Munich crisis in September 1938 when Britain hovered on the brink of war, a parents' meeting of the St Alban's schools discussed possible evacuation of their children to the countryside. The bombs that rained down on Highgate two years later continued the work of slum clearance. The schools nevertheless remained 'pretty full', as Dudley Clark told the parish: 'in fact it looks as though we might have to stop admitting any more to the junior and infants' school in the near future, as the accommodation is limited; one class room has to be kept as an air raid shelter.' The hardships of war continued afterwards with the intensification of rationing at home, partly to ensure the supply of food to Western Europe now free of German occupation. The consequences could be ironic. Six children from St Alban's joined a party of boys and girls from Birmingham secondary schools on a month of holiday arranged by the former resistance movement in Belgium; and nourished on Belgian cream, the students returned on average five to ten pounds heavier.

For schools, the most important event of the war was passage in 1944 of the Butler Education Act named after its sponsoring minister. The 1944 Act confirmed and amplified the institutional changes associated with raising the school leaving age to 15. Butler took care in preparatory conversations to involve the schools affiliated to the Church of England. Dudley Clark was encouraged by what he learned about the government's proposals before the Act was passed.

2. In the Wake of the Founders

The diocesan education authorities in Birmingham convened a meeting of all their school managers to outline the ramifications of the Act for church schools. Alongside the basic division of all state-funded schools between primary for children under the age of eleven and secondary for children thereafter, schools affiliated to the Church of England were to be classified as 'aided' or 'controlled' depending on the amount of financial support they received from church sources, 'aided' for those more generously supported, 'controlled' for the less.

The diocese encouraged St Alban's to become a voluntary aided secondary school. However flattering, there were several drawbacks to the recommendation. The managers of the school would have to shoulder heavy financial responsibilities to attain aided status. The cost of opening as a secondary school was estimated at £80,000 of which the managers would have to raise half. The diocese thought the St Alban's managers could raise this sum because of the school's endowments, mainly the Spenser bequest made during the First World War, supplemented by the generosity of affluent supporters of St Alban's Church. The ministry of education still sought guarantees that the managers could raise the requisite sum for a new building and an annual maintenance charge for each student; and the ministry continued to raise its financial requirements. Designation as a secondary school had another drawback for St Alban's because it involved removal of the primary department, the base of the original school and the major source of enrolment for the higher grades.

There was a third and most damaging drawback to the recommendations of the diocese for St Alban's. The Butler Act divided primary from secondary education with an examination of children at the age of eleven, and on the basis of that examination, again divided the provision of secondary education between grammar schools for the academically most able students and secondary modern schools to offer less demanding, more practical courses of study for the large, less gifted majority. The poverty of Highgate and the level of attainment of most of its students led the diocese to classify St Alban's as a secondary modern school. Children from Highgate who did well in the eleven plus examinations could proceed, as gifted students from St Alban's had always done, to a good grammar school elsewhere in the city. But designation as a secondary modern school implied low aspirations. Though that had never been true of the people of Highgate, St Alban's school would be lumbered with that reputation for the rest of the century.

While wrestling with these challenges, St Alban's lost two leaders of proven distinction. The death of John Goodman in 1952 deprived the school of its link to its founding years. He had served as manager of the school for more than half a century, carrying it through the dark years after the death of the Pollocks, providing it with crucial financial support, and helping to find work for the boys when they left school. The following year Dudley Clark died. Vicar of St Alban's for thirty years, he paid close attention to the school during its transformation with the raising of the school leaving age and passage of the Butler Education Act, a process now close to completion. Both men found able successors. John Goodman was followed by his daughter Mary who in 1957 became governor and then treasurer of the school. Dudley Clark's successor as vicar, Lawrence Harding, was to serve as vicar and manager of the school for almost as long and through a period of still greater turbulence.

St Alban's received a mixed report on the eve of its designation as a Church of England voluntary aided secondary modern school. The HMI censured its building and playground as inadequate, its lavatories as unsanitary, its ventilation bad, windows dirty, too few dustbins, too many children in attendance, no staff room. Despite these drawbacks, the inspector found that the school under its head teacher and staff was doing good work. The only explanation he could find for the willingness of the staff to serve amid bad working conditions was loyalty to the vicar and managers: in other words it was a religious commitment. That commitment was about to be challenged by further, more extensive slum clearance which accompanied the construction of a broad ring road or 'middleway' through the heart of Highgate, and the resulting social and religious reconstruction of the community.

Chapter 3

DUAL CHALLENGE: DEMOLITION AND THE DIOCESE

A variety of social and cultural forces converged on Highgate after the Second World War, turning it into a very different community from the one that the Pollocks had served. Its economic situation was not fundamentally changed. Highgate remained among the poorest inner-city wards in England. Yet it was more attractive and healthier than in the Pollocks' day. The new housing, blocks of flats and maisonettes, were cleaner than the back-to-backs they replaced; and most of the little workshops and factories that polluted the air in Victorian times were torn down or deserted, though their departure lessened the opportunities for employment within walking distance. The great change to Highgate in the 1950s and '60s came as the last back-to-backs were demolished and the families that they had housed were moved away from the city centre.

Enrolment at St Alban's school declined with every back-to-back that was demolished, and it could not rise before new housing could be constructed. The conversion of St Alban's into a secondary school made the enrolment problem more acute because a new school building had to be constructed to meet government standards; and the new building was designed for the increase in population that was expected once the new housing was fully occupied. There were no more than 284 students in the existing building in 1958 when it became a secondary school; and the new building would accommodate 450.

The fall in enrolment was nevertheless expected to be temporary. The enduring challenge for the school stemmed from cultural changes in the incoming population. The Pollocks had earned the respect of the community that grew up around their church and schools for their socially concerned Anglo-Catholicism. During the interwar years the people of Highgate remained familiar with the robed clergy, choir and congregation who processed along its streets on high days and holidays. The Christian impact of St Alban's church in Highgate was reinforced by Hope Street, later Highgate Baptist church on one side and St Anne's Roman Catholic church, where the Blessed John Henry Newman had once served, on the other. But many of the people who revered those traditions had moved away by 1960. The first signs of a difference among the incoming population were wrapped up with concern about falling enrolment at the school. The clergy discovered to their dismay that 'the parents of most children were apathetic about Church Schools'. The weakening of religious belief and rise of secularism across Western Europe was evident early in Highgate.

Lawrence Harding, the priest who in 1953 succeeded Dudley Clark as vicar of St Alban's, recognised the need for fresh thinking on the religious character of the school. But what impressed him was not the weakening of religious belief in Highgate but, on the contrary, the recently deepened commitment of the school to the Church of England when it won designation as a voluntary aided school. To secure that status, the Church had to pledge itself to a deep commitment of its financial resources for the next forty years. It received grants from several trusts, the National Society and individual donors to this end. The Parochial Church Council promised a substantial annual commitment in cooperation with the diocese, and the staff and children of the school added what they could.

Now called St Alban's CE School, the acquisition of voluntary aided status deepened concern about enrolment when in 1958 the Ministry of Education classified it as a secondary modern school. Enrolment was the first order of business for the newly constituted governing body of the school. It was chaired by Father Harding and included the director of the Diocesan Board of Education and a delegation from the parish church along with a representative of the City Council. Father Harding wanted St Alban's to become 'THE Church School of the Diocese'. He hoped to recruit children from Church of England families beyond Highgate. But the governor appointed by the Local Education Authority pointed out that the school would have to offer a very high standard of education to make it attractive outside Highgate. The head teacher, James Brandwood, added encouragingly that a high standard would attract teachers who might otherwise be uneasy about the academic quality of a secondary modern school. But Brandwood also pointed out that the requirement for teachers at St Alban's to subscribe to its religious affiliation, strongly though he endorsed it, made recruiting able staff more difficult.

To push the discussion forward, he outlined the options for the school. It could continue to focus its attention on the local community; but in that case, he added bluntly, 'the general level of intelligence will continue to be low and the standard remain likewise.' He did not expect more than the occasional unusually bright student locally to gain entry to a grammar school elsewhere. And no one yet conceived of the possibility that St Alban's might lift most of its students up to grammar school levels of attainment. The alternative that Father Harding favoured was for the school to recruit students throughout the deanery and diocese on the basis of their allegiance to the Church of England. 'In this case,' Brandwood commented, 'it will be easy to raise the cultural tone of the School. Pupils may then be encouraged to stay on for a 5th Year with profit and the academic future would appear much brighter.' He nevertheless put forward a third option, providing a fixed number of places for church children and then filling it up with local children.

The governors did not settle on any of these options and instead waited during construction of the new building to see where the student intake came from. The location for the new building emphasized its religious affiliation for it was placed across the street from the vicarage and parish church. Here the school would remain for nearly half a century. It opened encouragingly in 1965 with 342 students, its highest enrolment in eight years. Provision was made for more as families moved into the new housing by keeping two classrooms without plastering.

But the anticipated rise failed to materialise. On the contrary, the intake in 1967 fell. Brandwood deepened the governors' disappointment by pointing out that the entering class came in with an exceptionally low standard of attainment. Letters were despatched to surrounding primary schools to attract their children to St Alban's, and the intake rose the following year. But a year later Brandwood drew attention to another feature of the enrolment at St Alban's that placed the religious aspirations of the school in jeopardy. The Church of England primary schools in the neighbourhood were finding it necessary to fill their classrooms with children of other religious affiliations, to begin with Roman Catholics from the nearby Irish population.

At the end of the decade Brandwood alerted the governors in strictest confidence to another 'very delicate matter' that accentuated the religious diversity of the locality. The Local Education Authority had asked him to admit enough children from the Immigration Centres in the city to meet the minimum intake required of St Alban's. When he completed his school register for the coming year, he 'found that I had on roll some 54 immigrant children of whom approximately half were non-Christian. In addition, I have some 50 children in School of the Roman Catholic Faith. This brings the total of non-Anglican children in the School to over 100' or nearly thirty per cent of the total. Brandwood went on to point out that 'Some of our non-Christian children in recent years turned out to be some of our best pupils but', he added, 'this does not alter the fact that S. Albans is a C/E Aided Secondary School whose aim should be to give the children a sound Christian Education in the Anglican Tradition.' He concluded, 'may I repeat that this is certainly not a question of race or colour but of creed only.' Highgate was becoming one of the most ethnically diverse inner-city wards in the country. The immigrants who moved into the new housing came to England ambitious to improve their lot including the education of their children. But how could a committed Church of England school respond to their hopes?

That question was to divide vicars of the parish church from the diocesan Directors of Religious Education for nearly twenty years. The challenge no longer came from the rise of religious indifference and secularism in the community but of strong but differing religious convictions. An improvement in enrolment and in the financial position at St Alban's School deferred the debate for a few years. With 520 pupils on roll by 1973 as the new housing was occupied, there were in fact too many for a building designed to accommodate 450. At the same time the school governors and parish church were able to use the proceeds from no longer needed property to reimburse the diocese completely for its contribution to the construction costs of the new building. The voluntary aided status that financial support for the school had acquired also enabled it to curb an effort by the Local Education Authority, now under Labour control, to push all the schools in the city into a common mould through consortia.

St Alban's School needed help from neighbouring schools, however, in another regard. Labour had launched an attempt when it came to power nationally in 1964 to overcome the invidious distinction between grammar and secondary modern schools by combining students of all levels of ability in comprehensive schools. When the Local Education Authority came under Labour control, it insisted, as the new head teacher at St Alban's, the Rev. W.H. Roberts, told the governors, that all comprehensive schools 'must have reasonable "A" level provision since a school lacking in this respect is liable to have inadequate standing in the community.' Roberts hammered the message home. St Alban's was 'only just coping with "O" level courses.' It would take a lot of hard work and cooperation with neighbouring schools to introduce "A" levels. But failure to do so would turn St Alban's into a 'sink' school. Roberts was able to report progress the next year, with enrolment up to 553 and 21 in the 6th form: 'we hope that they will be an asset to the school.'

The skies darkened in 1980. The block of flats with which Highgate had experimented before the war was poorly constructed, as was so often the case with social housing, and in any case the residents longed to transfer from tower blocks into maisonettes. So another spate of demolition struck the community, and enrolment at St Alban's School resumed its fall. The fall looked all the more serious because the school-age population of Birmingham generally was expected to decline throughout the decade. The economic outlook for the West Midlands deepened the gloom. Manufacturing industry upon which the prosperity of the region depended was devastated by the monetarist financial policy adopted by the recently elected Thatcher government, and unemployment skyrocketed. The combination of a falling school-age population and falling financial resources placed the Local Education Authority in a tight squeeze. Education accounted for 60 per cent of the city's budget, and there were 18,000 empty places in the city's schools. Highgate, always among the poorest parts of the city, felt the pinch acutely. The community was further saddened in the spring of 1981 by the death of the much loved vicar, Father Harding.

There was no time to mourn. The head teacher and interim chair of the governors of St Alban's were summoned to a meeting with the heads and chairs of the other two Church of England secondary schools in central Birmingham, Lea Mason and St George's, Newtown, to acquaint them with discussions going on in the Local Education Authority. The over-supply of schools was particularly glaring in these three Church of England schools, all with low enrolment. St

Alban's had the lowest of the three. But it had compensating advantages: as a voluntary aided school, it had substantial financial support and powers to protect its autonomy, support and power the other two 'controlled' CE schools lacked. Similar discussion about the future of the three church schools went on in the Diocesan Board of Education, but the leaders of St Alban's School were not invited to it.

From the outset, the Local Education Authority (LEA) and the Diocesan Board of Education (DBE) reacted differently to the over-supply of inner-city schools in a period of economic depression. The LEA was reluctant to close schools in poor central wards and decided to leave all secondary schools in the city on hold for another three or four years. But the diocese was unwilling to retain three secondary schools in the central parts of the city where church congregations were small, smaller than in the affluent suburbs. The DBE wanted to amalgamate St Alban's and Lea Mason but was deterred by the difficulty of uniting an aided with a controlled school. The Diocesan Director of Education instructed St Alban's to keep a low profile and refrain from raising questions with the LEA and meanwhile to use the next few years to 'prove itself'.

Though St Alban's began 1982 with an enrolment well over four hundred, the predicted fall in the school-age population and depressing economic news in the city as a whole led the staff, students and parents to expect the closure of the school sooner or later. Two appointments that February, however, brought St Alban's a fighting chance of survival. David Hutt came from a school chaplaincy at Kings College, Taunton, to become vicar of St Alban's. He came, as he said, because of the school; and he turned out to be the first vicar of St Alban's since the Pollocks to treat the school as equal in importance to the parish church. Indeed Father Hutt believed that, in view of the changing religious complexion of Highgate and the now largely non-resident congregation of the parish church, the church depended upon the school to meet its pastoral obligations to the parish. In other words, without the school, the parish church would wither and die. Father Hutt was seconded by the appointment of Councillor Richard Knowles as LEA governor of the school. Knowles was as staunchly Anglo-Catholic in his churchmanship as he was Labour in his politics, and he was about to become leader of Labour on the council. He re-embodied the social gospel of the Oxford Movement that Father Tom Pollock had personified.

3. Dual Challenge: Demolition and the Diocese

Father Hutt was thrown into battle for the school upon arrival when he received a letter from the Bishop of Birmingham. The bishop had stayed out of the preceding discussions but now said that he wanted to transfer St Alban's voluntary aided status and, if possible, its money to Lea Mason where the two schools would be consolidated. He proposed asking the Chief Education Officer of the city to prepare a notice of closure for St Alban's; and he gave Father Hutt a few days to respond.

The new vicar marshalled his forces before responding. He received lukewarm response from the already demoralised teaching staff of the school. They favoured amalgamation with the Lea Mason staff to meet the changing curricular needs of the community particularly in foreign languages. The leadership of Lea Mason did not, however, welcome amalgamation, while the governors of St Alban's fully supported Hutt's determination to put up 'a big fight'. They agreed that 'it was their moral responsibility to continue Christian instruction' in Highgate 'and not to give away their inheritance and stewardship' through amalgamation with the school in another community.

Emphasising that the school was founded 'to serve the immediate needs of the people living in S. Alban's parish,' Hutt decided to rally support at a public meeting; and only then did he reply to the bishop. The crowd of nearly two hundred that packed the school gave him enthusiastic support. Its closure, said one St Alban's school parent, 'would be like tearing the heart out of the community.' A reporter for the *Sunday Mercury* (14 Mar 1982) was surprised to discover in Highgate 'a sense of – or perhaps a craving for – the feeling of living in a village, where people are close-knit and caring.' Another St Alban's mother told him 'It's the kind of school where whole families go. Parents, grandparents, cousins and so on.' She had five children all of whom had gone to St Alban's, were there now or intended to go. 'I was married in St Alban's Church and the children were christened and confirmed there.' Lea Mason, she explained, was too far away and would involve many youngsters having to make their way across the dangerously busy Pershore, Belgrave and Bristol Roads. She valued the comprehensive nature of the education her children received at St Alban's. 'One of my children left last year with 10 "O" levels … and you can't complain about that. Another of my kids left with no exam passes at all but she has never been out of work. … They show the children all aspects of life, including how to cope with the dole and unemployment.'

Between church and mosque, the view from St Alban's CE School at the end of the twentieth century.

Hutt secured further favourable publicity from the local press. Under a banner headline of '**Parish v. church in fight over school**', the *Evening Mail* reported admiringly about the campaign of 'a vicar who only arrived a month ago.' Hutt likened his fight to David versus Goliath: 'It is not a great school,' he said, 'it is small, but it serves the needs of the community.' He addressed those needs 'particularly in a time of high unemployment' by opening the school after hours for community use. He presented the choice in stark terms: it was either closure by the city as recommended by the bishop or the overturning of that recommendation by appeal to the Secretary of State for Education in London. To follow up, Hutt formed an Action Group with Dick Knowles as consultant and announced that all other work in the church would be suspended until the future of the school was decided. Thereupon the bishop beat a retreat: 'there is no immediate threat of closure of St. Alban's School,' he assured Father Hutt sheepishly: '… thank you all for a wonderful effort in drawing the attention of the press and the general public to our determination to preserve the school for this area. We have in Councillor Dick Knowles a good friend and ally.'

But the battle was far from over. The LEA issued new proposals for secondary school reorganisation which retained both St Alban's and Lea Mason 'subject to

3. Dual Challenge: Demolition and the Diocese

discussion with the Diocesan Authorities.' The gravity of the situation was nonetheless borne in upon St Alban's by the closure because of dwindling numbers of its sister primary school, St Patrick's. Father Hutt sought support wherever he could find it. Though uneasy about the expanding Muslim presence in Highgate, he adapted the religious teaching at the school to the changes in the community 'to present, without compromise, Christian teaching especially as there is a minority of Christians at the school and at the same time show regard for other faiths in the school.' He joined the students and staff regularly for lunch. The staff nevertheless continued to press for amalgamation with Lea Mason. This pressure brought to the surface discontent with the head teacher, Margery Turner, who ran the school without much reference to the staff. Before the summer term ended, she conceded that a staff meeting would be held at the beginning of the new school year, that there would be a minimum of two staff meetings each term, monthly meetings with heads of departments, and a short staff briefing at the beginning of each week.

The New Year brought new troubles. Enrolment continued to decline, falling below 400. Hutt turned again for help to the community. 'We have to make the School a Community as well as a Church School,' he said, 'a unique position in this sort of area.' Dick Knowles drew attention to a related change in the demands upon the city from the Birmingham Central Mosque that towered over one side of Highgate: 'tremendous pressure,' Knowles reported, 'was put on the Moslem Councillors by the older Moslem men, that their women were becoming more and more Westernised and that they wanted their daughters to attend Girls' Schools from the age of 12, to prevent this.' St Alban's had educated boys and girls separately until it was turned into a secondary modern school, but to transform it back into a girls' school under Muslim pressure could negate its founding purpose. At the same time the LEA secured approval for its reorganisation of Birmingham schools under which one of its secondary schools in the Highgate area would be turned into a sixth form college, and St Alban's would have to close its sixth form. That loss would deprive St Alban's of any academic lustre it had retained, turning it into the 'sink' school which the former head master, Roberts, had dreaded. Thus the LEA, in spite of its claim to favour retention of small schools in poor areas, undermined St Alban's by fostering the growth of a nearby rival. After eighteen months of hard work, Father Hutt was as fearful of the closure of St Alban's as he had been on arrival.

The battle lines hardened with the appointment of a new Diocesan Director of Education, Richard Lindley. Interest in a single-sex school for Muslim girls took firmer shape with an offer to buy St Alban's school for this purpose. The question of its future was further accentuated when Margery Turner gave notice of her intention to retire. Meanwhile Dick Knowles' ability to speak up for the school was enhanced when Labour gained power at the local elections and he became Leader of the Council; but he now had other demanding duties. Father Hutt accordingly brought another Anglo-Catholic Labour supporter who sat on the city's Education Committee, Bryan Stoten, onto the governing body to reinforce Knowles. It was Stoten who replied for the school when Lindley summarised the stance of the diocese. Determined to reduce the Church's provision of secondary schooling in the centre of the city, Lindley insisted on some form of amalgamation with Lea Mason, either by setting up a split site school on both locations or by transferring the name, voluntary aided status and financial assets of St Alban's to Lea Mason, putting the school land and building in Highgate up for sale. Lindley recognised the opportunity this would provide for the establishment of a Muslim school there. He proved willing to do much to accommodate the expanding Muslim presence in Highgate, more than Father Hutt. Though Hutt encouraged the school to inculcate respect for all religious faiths in Highgate, he reacted uneasily to the predominance there of a religion alien to English traditions.

Before responding to Lindley, Stoten spoke to the leading figures on education in the city as well as the diocese to pinpoint the source of the pressure to close St Alban's. Trudy Livingstone who chaired the pertinent education sub-committee of the city dwelt on the importance of maintaining small secondary schools in the inner city, and she also expressed concern at the prospect of the Islamic community setting up its own independent school. Her response enabled Stoten to discredit the diocesan attempt to pass responsibility for the closure of either of the CE secondary schools at issue on to the city; and Knowles as Leader of the Council offered to convey the same unwelcome message to the Bishop of Birmingham. Stoten nevertheless appreciated the significance of the deficiencies in the curriculum offered by St Alban's, and he called for speedy introduction of Urdu or Arabic. He also pressed for widened representation from the Highgate community on the governing body of St Alban's and called for the appointment

3. Dual Challenge: Demolition and the Diocese

of Paul Walker, recently appointed minister at Highgate Baptist Church, and a representative from the Central Mosque as governors. Hutt strengthened Stoten's hand by securing support from the chairman of the trustees of St Alban's who controlled the assets of the school to refuse to transfer them to Lea Mason.

Hesitantly and uneasily, opinions began to converge around the establishment of a girls' school under the voluntary aided aegis of St Alban's where the Christian creed of the Church of England would be taught along with respect for all the other creeds in the community including Sikhs and Hindus as well as Muslims. Lindley was unenthusiastic because this plan would allow St Alban's to survive without amalgamation; and he pleaded for delay. But the governors gave the plan a warmer welcome: 'In the context of the inner city and the meeting of many faiths,' they noted, 'a Voluntary Aided School has a unique opportunity to act as a bridge-builder.' With an eye on immigration from the West Indies, Knowles heralded 'a glorious opportunity for the Christian Church to serve this area and remain faithful to the Christian service.' With some confidence that St Alban's could survive along these lines, David Hutt accepted promotion from St Alban's to the leading Anglo-Catholic church in London, All Saints, Margaret Street.

The city's education committee proceeded to petition the Secretary of State to turn St Alban's into a single-sex school. But the proposal ran into immediate opposition. Selly Park Girls School reacted with dismay, and two teachers unions, the NUT and the NASUWT, came out against the change as a threat to the neighbouring schools. The St Alban's staff added to the protests, fearful that in practice a single-sex school in Highgate would cater exclusively for Muslim girls. The governors of St Alban's also drew back because the petition of the city's education committee ignored the issue of religious affiliation and would involve reconstituting the governing body. Without needing to say why, the Secretary of State rejected the city's petition.

This rejection put the school back in limbo, uncertain how to secure its future and where its support lay. The new vicar Michael Bryant gave the school what support he could, and the governors remained staunch. The new head teacher Sheila Lyman sought to turn the obvious weaknesses of the school, its low enrolment and low level of student attainment, into assets by focusing attention on students with special needs, whether because of their poverty or because English was not their native language. This approach won a sympathetic response from the LEA and Lindley. But it was shot down by an HMI inspection in 1989. While the inspector recognised that 60 per cent of the students did not have English as their first language and that 57 per cent were eligible for free school meals, he criticised the school for underestimating the ability of the pupils. The reading tasks presented to the pupils were, he said, too structured and simplified, and in mathematics too much reliance was placed on pocket calculators instead of encouraging mental arithmetic. Sheila Lyman responded robustly to this critique. But in doing so she accepted the hitherto universal assumption that children in a poor immigrant community were unlikely to reach high levels of educational attainment. The 1989 HMI report on St Alban's marked an important precedent by challenging that belief.

However unfamiliar, this criticism undermined support for the school on the pertinent sub-committee of the City Council and did nothing to gain sympathy for the school from the Diocesan Education Council. One member of the sub-committee, Councillor Eames from Small Heath, questioned the worth of a school with a mere 228 students on its roll, half of what it had in 1978; and a year later it fell to 221. Eames spoke only for himself, and the chairman of the full Education Committee sought to reassure Sheila Lyman by praising the strong pastoral tradition at St Alban's and the high standards of behaviour of its students; but he did not refute the HMI critique. And St Alban's found itself at the bottom of the list of GCSE results for all Birmingham schools the next year. Meanwhile the school came under assault from the Diocesan Education Council. It came out in favour of extending the remit of St George's, Newtown, currently the largest CE secondary school in central Birmingham, to cover the whole of that area, and the closure of either Lea Mason or St Alban's. When Richard Lindley embraced this recommendation, Bryan Stoten exploded, 'I am heartily sick of the Church of England demoralising its own staff and the morale in its own schools.'

A rumour that the diocese would provide a free bus service from Highgate to St George's, Newtown, set off alarm bells at St Alban's, a fear that slightly rising enrolment and improving student performance did nothing to allay. The diocese kept St Alban's in the dark about its intentions. The school was also anxious about the intentions of the city which was still trying to rid itself of 6,000 spare secondary school places. And in July 1992, the Diocesan Board of Education decided to keep two secondary schools open, one in the suburbs and one in the inner city. The axe that had hung over St Alban's for the past fifteen years seemed about to fall.

Unexpectedly, however, Lindley deflected it by developing a proposal from Sheila Lyman to focus St Alban's on children with special needs. In this way the school might attract children with special needs outside Highgate and beyond the centre of the city and thus increase its enrolment perhaps only modestly but enough to ensure survival. Lindley was beginning to suspect that the powers of resistance that voluntary aided status gave the governors of St Alban's and the financial resources which their longstanding treasurer, Mary Goodman, and her brother John who chaired the trustees had built up might in the end defeat his attempts to amalgamate and close the school. He offered accordingly to cooperate in drafting a statement to express the ethos and principles that underlay its focus on special needs. The statement spoke of 'bringing together the different cultural and religious groups in an environment where mutual respect and understanding can grow'. Toward that end the school offered to provide an induction course on English as a second language, to strengthen links with the city's Travelling Children Support Unit, and to build up its learning support staff. The statement concluded proudly, 'The school has a long history of working with some of the most deprived children in the city. Many have had erratic educational experience and have failed consistently. They are frequently successful because the school is small and particularly supportive. Through its special nature St Alban's represents an important and irreplaceable contribution to its local community, and a unique resource for the city at large.' The governors endorsed this statement with relief, and the Diocesan Board of Education concurred. Enrolment began to rise as parents of children with special needs across the city applied for admission. St Alban's won a reprieve.

But the reprieve was very brief, threatened this time by the city. Within a matter of weeks, the Education Committee put forward a proposal to merge St Alban's with two nearby secondary schools under LEA control. Sheila Lyman hastened to convene yet another public meeting to rally support for St Alban's, and parents and the local community as well as governors responded handsomely. But a strategy of reliance for survival on children with special needs had crucial drawbacks. There was little or no special funding for children with special needs. 'Applications for places for pupils continue to flood in,' Sheila Lyman reported, 'but alas, resources to help children who have special needs in terms of behaviour are never available.' Concentration on special needs also did nothing to address the main criticism in the recent HMI report on St Alban's that it underestimated the ability of its students and failed to raise attainment. The school came up with a development plan that attempted to combine service of special needs with raising attainment: it promised to create 'a stimulating environment where high standards are expected, and a wide range of relevant experiences is provided through which all pupils have equal opportunities to develop fully their varied talents'. Regardless of these words, St Alban's examination results remained among the lowest in the city. In 1994/5 only 7 per cent of St Alban's students achieved five or more passing grades of A to C in the GCSEs as compared to the citywide average of 32 per cent. Enrolment at St Alban's continued slowly to rise, protecting the school against precipitate amalgamation or closure. But its survival in the longer term remained in doubt.

To considerable surprise, once again Richard Lindley came to the aid of the school, this time more substantially, by pledging financial support from the diocese for the construction of a technology wing to enhance the curriculum. The rising proportion of students at St Alban's for whom English was a second language suggested that their talents might be better developed with a curriculum that stressed numeracy and various fields of technology. But that required dedicated teaching space and equipment. When the plans for a technology block were rejected by the Department for Education in London, Lindley encouraged the school to apply again. There were other causes of concern at St Alban's. Turnover in the immigrant community and hence at the school ran high as those who did well strove to move to more promising areas farther out in the city; and their departure depressed the school's GCSE results. Moreover families particularly from Pakistan, who accounted for more than half of the students at St Alban's, took their children back for prolonged stretches in their homeland, pulling the rate of attendance at the school below 80 per cent.

In the spring of 1996 light dawned, however, in the surprising form of another HMI report, this time in the name of the recently established Office of Standards in Education (Ofsted). It announce that 'St Alban's CE School has

3. Dual Challenge: Demolition and the Diocese

successfully emerged from a period of several years' – it should have said nearly twenty – 'in which its future was in doubt and the number of pupils fell to about 220. The roll has now risen to approach its full capacity, standards have risen, and the head teacher, governors and staff have established a learning environment in which pupils are cared for, relationships are good, and courtesy, tolerance and respect for a wide range of cultures, traditions and religions are given high priority.' This was not a dawn that the founders of the school could have envisioned. Deeply though the Pollocks had taken the destitution of Highgate to heart, the community they served in the nineteenth century was formed by immigration from much shorter distances and with much less diversity than the successor community at the end of the twentieth century. The dawn that Ofsted described in 1996 nevertheless reflected the still Anglo-Catholic social vision that inspired David Hutt, Dick Knowles and those who had fought alongside them over the past two decades to save the school. They had developed a vision that enabled a dedicated Church of England school to serve one of the neediest and ethnically most diverse inner-city wards in England. Yet it failed to raise the attainment of students in Highgate to the level that the Department of Education was beginning nationally to demand.

Chapter 4

RECOVERING IN EXCEPTIONALLY CHALLENGING CIRCUMSTANCES

The Ofsted report of 1996 balanced its praise of the school's achievement with an outline in critical detail of how far it had yet to go to guarantee its survival. As Sheila Lyman summed it up, 'the school still faces big challenges before it will be able to come out of the "serious weakness" category.' Though both the Diocesan Board of Education and the Local Education Authority supported the governors in exploring ways to secure the long term viability of the school, closure remained all too possible. The close-knit community of the back-to-backs had long gone, replaced by a very mixed community of aspiring immigrants and the downwardly mobile. There were nevertheless heartening changes in the local and national leadership. Tim Brighouse took charge as chief education officer in Birmingham with policies encouraging schools to improve rather than damning them for their shortcomings. Richard Lindley retired as diocesan Director of Education, and his successor, while still uneasy about St Alban's, proved less hostile. Hopes ran high nationally the following spring when a New Labour government was elected, committed above all to 'Education, education, education'.

Regardless of its final assessment, Ofsted had found more to criticise about the school than to praise. Like all the inspectors who visited St Alban's, Ofsted praised it for 'promoting the spiritual, moral and social development of pupils.' Its main strength otherwise, said Ofsted, lay in its leadership and management: 'Now the school has a sense of purpose, clearly expressed in the statement of aims contained in the school brochure, and there is a commitment on the part of the head and staff to improve the quality of education and standards of achievement.' But in actuality the school fell far short of these aspirations. Its worst feature was in student attendance which averaged barely 70 per cent, a problem aggravated by a 35 per cent rate of student turnover. Highgate housed an immigrant population with one of the highest rates of inflow and outflow in the country. Tower blocks built in the 1960s and now largely abandoned by long-term tenants provided short-term housing for asylum seekers. Three quarters of the people of Highgate belonged to ethnic minorities. And they came to the poorest part of one of the ten most deprived wards in the country. The proportion of pupils qualifying for free school meals soared in two years from 45 to 72 per cent.

In face of these bleak statistics, Ofsted's commentary on the quality of teaching at St Alban's was disturbing. Though in four fifths of classes the teaching was judged sound or better, only half were deemed good. Provision for pupils with special needs or English as a second language, the groups on which the school concentrated its attention, varied in quality from just satisfactory to clearly inadequate. Little wonder that the GCSE results at St Alban's fell well below the national average. In 1996 only 4 per cent of pupils achieved 5 or more A-C grades; and results in the basic subjects of English, mathematics and science were particularly poor.

The head teacher responded by insisting that 'results must improve especially in the core subjects.' But the targets she set in the School Development Plan were far from ambitious: 2 per cent more A-C GCSE grades, reduction in the number of students leaving without any GCSE passes at all, and alternative certification in more subjects for those unable to take GCSEs. With 299 of its 388 students on the SEN register in 1998, St Alban's remained the 'sink' school that W.H. Roberts had dreaded. The dividends of its focus on special needs disappeared as the Labour government adopted a policy of inclusion in the mainstream for all but a small minority of pupils, a policy Birmingham under Brighouse embraced with enthusiasm. On the other hand, Labour promised differential funding to assist schools in deprived areas – and St Alban's would come top on that reckoning. The other bright spot for the school came with the refurbished technology wing for which Mark Higgins, the new head of technology, secured good equipment.

When Sheila Lyman retired in the last year of the century, Ofsted praised her 'effective, decisive and positive leadership and management'. In the three years since the last inspection, the school had moved out of the category of Serious

Weaknesses, with higher standards of teaching and support for pupils and better levels of attendance. But the level of attainment among the students remained far below the national average. Ofsted provided a comprehensive list of the school's continuing weaknesses: in literacy skills, EAL support (with more than thirty first languages), vocational education at Key Stage 4, independent learning skills, support for SEN, and consistent assessment. The governors sought a committed Christian for head teacher, drawing attention to the multi-faith dimensions of the school; and they selected the deputy head, David Gould.

He moved swiftly to address the weaknesses that Ofsted pointed out. But he began by establishing the style of directive but pervasively collective leadership that became his trademark. He set up a Senior Leadership Team (SLT) of three, a Pastoral Leadership Team of the three heads of years, and a Curriculum Leadership Team of the subject leaders. He submitted a bid for the creation of an Education Action Zone (EAZ) in Highgate, an initiative by the Labour government to help schools set up local networks of schools for mutual support and shared resources. With a view to raising attainment, he sought to appoint a Gifted and Talented Pupils coordinator.

He then drafted a Post-Inspection Action Plan that matched, point by point, the areas of concern identified by Ofsted: literacy levels, vocational courses for pupils for whom GCSEs were not appropriate, independent learning skills through use of the library, coordination of SEN, and a consistent marking and assessment policy. The diocese rallied to his support with a grant of £50,000 for a learning centre based around the library to serve the community as well as the school. By the end of the year St Alban's was setting the pace in school improvement according to a new School Improvement Index which showed a national average rate of 10 per cent and a Birmingham average rate of 20 per cent with St Alban's at 26.4. At the beginning of the new century, enrolment at St Alban's passed 400. But attendance remained disappointing despite the appointment of a member of staff to contact all families on the first day of an absence from school. Even more disappointing was the failure to raise the number of students receiving GCSEs with 5 grades of A to C. And the Key Stage 3 results in English were down from the previous year.

Right: Head teachers of the Octet schools with the Schools Minister, David Miliband.

4. Recovering in Exceptionally Challenging Circumstances

Both the pace that David Gould set and the disappointing results were reflected in an invitation he received after eighteen months as head teacher to attend a conference in London for well managed schools facing exceptional challenges in deprived areas. The invitation turned out to be more significant than he initially appreciated. He found that St Alban's was one of eight secondary schools selected to participate in what came to be known as the Octet project. Generously funded by the Labour government, it sought to develop, refine and test a model of intervention and improvement aimed at schools in some of the most difficult socio-economic contexts in England. The schools were chosen on the basis of their poor examination results, economic deprivation measured by the proportion of students on free school meals, and the high quality of their leadership. The eight schools were to draw up individual education plans for each student, to focus on literacy and numeracy, and to give teachers more time to plan and assess work together and to share best practice. The LEA in Birmingham added further support and funding for schools in the city including St Alban's that were a cause for concern.

St Alban's used the Octet project to shift its emphasis from special needs to high expectations. An extra hour for literacy and numeracy was added to the entry year timetable. The Senior Leadership Team was strengthened with the expansion of its membership to five including two experienced teachers from other schools in the city to help with curricular development, behaviour

management, data tracking and strategic leadership. Performance management of teachers was tightened and tied to pay increases. Mark Higgins joined the leadership group to give St Alban's a specialism in engineering, remarkably the first secondary school to bid for that distinction in Birmingham whose wealth was based on metal manufacturing. To build on the strength of its existing provision in technology, St Alban's deepened its cooperation with the nearby further education provider, Matthew Boulton College.

The Octet project set the pace of improvement in its participating schools by asking Ofsted to inspect them every six months. The initial report on St Alban's identified its gravest weakness and gave it clear direction. The standards that St Alban's students reached by the end of Key Stage 4 were very low in terms not only of national averages but also of similarly challenged schools. They were the lowest of the Octet eight. Poor levels of attainment had long been the case at St Alban's; but the school had comforted itself with the praise it had always received on the behaviour of its students. Ofsted, however, found good behaviour in barely half of the classes inspected, better undoubtedly than in many schools but not exemplary. More gratifying was the report that the quality of teaching was satisfactory or better in all but two lessons and good or better in more than half. Attendance was edging upwards, approaching 90 per cent. The appointment of two additional assistant head teachers enabled the head to blend all the initiatives, funding streams and action plans into a clear, simple vision to which everyone in the school could subscribe. Ofsted insisted that 'The focus always needs to be on raising standards.'

In its next report, Ofsted took issue with what the school had considered one of its attractions, its treatment of students with special educational needs. The school had expanded its focus on this area by jumbling EAL students, some of them very bright, together with students with severe disabilities. The inspectors also found able students placed in low-ability groups because they were badly behaved. Ofsted accordingly called for a strategic overhaul to differentiate between these groups of students and provide them with teaching appropriate to their need and ability.

Though the school found these frequent inspections burdensome, the improving results were gratifying: in September 2002 the percentage of students who received 5 A*-C grades in the GCSEs rose into double figures, the results at

Key Stage 3 (KS3) were the best ever, and the school was filled to capacity with 432 students on its roll. Meanwhile St Alban's extended its range of institutional partnerships. They had begun with Matthew Boulton College in engineering. Then the Highgate Education Action Zone was established to foster cooperation with a broad circle of primary schools. St Alban's established a close relationship with St Peter's Collegiate CE School and Technology College in Wolverhampton, a successful secondary school in a privileged social setting quite different from Highgate from which both schools benefitted. St Alban's also welcomed the addition of value added data to the national league tables on KS3 and GCSE results where St Alban's stood at or near the bottom. The local press took delight in headlining the KS3 results at St Alban's as '**Worst in Country**'. But on the new value added index which marked the degree of improvement in each school, the national figure at KS4 was 100 and for Birmingham was 99.3 but St Alban's reached a high of 102.4.

While recognising signal improvement, the Ofsted report in the spring of 2003 contained some sobering observations. The KS3 results in English had improved dramatically. But the results in mathematics and science remained well below those of similarly challenged schools, and the quality of teaching in science was particularly poor. The proportion of pupils achieving five higher grade GCSEs and of pupils achieving at least one GCSE also remained well below that of similar schools including the others in the Octet project. Continuing problems with student behaviour were reflected in a high level of exclusions, and the target of 90 per cent in attendance remained elusive. Ofsted commended the Senior Leadership Team on its growing confidence and expertise. But the school had not made much headway in its use of assessment data and target setting for individual students. The Octet project was nevertheless congratulated for helping the school to make improvements at a faster rate than would otherwise be possible. Funding for the project was extended for another year and was supplemented by other Labour government grants to schools in challenging circumstances.

There was much to crow about that autumn. 19 per cent of the students taking their GCSEs received 5 A*-Cs, just short of the national average. Letters of congratulation poured in from the Bishop of Birmingham, the Chief Education Officer for the city, and the Head of the Standards and Effectiveness

Unit at the Department for Education and Skills in London. But the KS3 results were much lower than in the previous year for all core subjects, a fall attributed to the particularly low level of attainment on entry that year but still disappointing; and attendance remained unsatisfactory. The quality of teaching and learning was improving across the school particularly in literacy; there was also improvement in the performance of middle managers; and support for SEN and EAL, areas of recent concern, was now good. Throughout the school there was a welcome shift in priorities from concern about the wellbeing of the students toward concern about their academic performance. After a critical assessment in the spring of the year, the governance of the school was strengthened with the establishment of a committee system. Ofsted saw need for further development in the leadership skills of the head and deputy head teachers, in the use of data to improve teaching, and at KS3 in literacy, numeracy and ICT. In its final report under the Octet project, Ofsted nevertheless lifted St Alban's out of the danger zone and ranked its performance as 'satisfactory'.

'Satisfactory' did not guarantee survival. With 430 students on its roll, St Alban's was dangerously small for a secondary school; yet there was no room for more within its existing walls. Though its GCSE and KS3 results continued upward, they remained below the national norm. The quality of teaching and learning at the school was still its weakest feature. The Octet project had been more concerned about the exceptionally challenging circumstances that its participating schools faced than about enabling children in those circumstances to reach high levels of academic attainment.

St Alban's took several signal steps forward as the Octet project reached its conclusion. With backing from the National Grid, Cadbury's, United Fleet and BMW and in cooperation with St Peter's Collegiate in Wolverhampton, Matthew Boulton College and Aston University, the school secured specialist status in engineering. That status gave St Alban's £150,000 in capital resources pertinent to engineering; and while heightened emphasis was placed on mathematics, science and technology, interest in engineering percolated through the entire curriculum. The Highgate Education Action Zone facilitated cooperation with neighbouring primary schools who for the first time provided more than half of the intake into St Alban's. Its student body thus grew more cohesive than in the days when it depended on the admission of troubled students drawn from more than thirty primaries across the city. St Alban's also gave a lead in the Central Collegiate Academy, a consortium of secondary schools in the heart of Birmingham formed to share their individual strengths with each other.

Still, so long as the school remained within its existing walls, it could not expand to securely viable proportions. Here again the Labour government provided the way forward with a lavishly funded programme of Building Schools for the Future (BSF). The Local Authority in Birmingham envisaged an expansion of the enrolment at St Alban's to 600. Hopes soared at the school. Because BSF gave priority to areas of economic deprivation, St Alban's expected to be ranked among the first in Birmingham to receive a new building. But in the ranking by Birmingham's LEA, St Alban's kept slipping into the second category, perhaps because as a voluntary aided Church of England school it was not entirely a city concern. Whatever caused the slippage, the head teacher and chair of governors of the school looked anxiously for a way to secure its expansion and survival.

Chapter 5

EXTENDING FAITH IN THE INNER CITY

The destitution of Highgate in the mid-nineteenth century ignited the Anglo-Catholic social vision of the Pollock brothers in founding St Alban's School. That vision was institutionalised in the mid-twentieth century at St Alban's with its acquisition of voluntary aided status and substantial endowment as a Church of England school, status and wealth that saved it from closure toward the end of the century. While remaining true to that vision, the head teacher and chair of governors sought to integrate it with an expansion of the school that would enable it not only to survive but flourish in the twenty-first century. The enrolment of 600 that Birmingham city planners envisaged was barely enough for survival. To do well and really distinguish itself, St Alban's would need to open a sixth form, building on its specialism in engineering, and expand to 800. The schools minister in the Labour government, Andrew Adonis, offered St Alban's a way to achieve this in cooperation with the educational charity ARK (Absolute Return for Kids). The process that the schools minister thus opened up moved slowly to begin with and proved difficult. Although ARK stressed its lack of religious affiliation, it had its own faith in the inner city. It insisted that children in poor inner-city neighbourhoods could be brought to levels of attainment in education as high as those reached in affluent suburbs. Eventually the fusion of the ARK faith with the faith of the school's founders produced outstanding results.

The evidence that St Alban's had slipped in the city's ranking of schools for a new building under the BSF programme was accompanied by talk of St Alban's acquiring 'Academy status'. The creation of 'academies' stood at the heart of a campaign by the schools minister to deal with the failure of many comprehensive

5. Extending Faith in the Inner City

secondary schools to give their students an education good enough for them to earn their living and contribute usefully to the community. There was considerable uncertainty at this early stage of the campaign as to what becoming an academy would entail; but it opened another route to early BSF funding. Discussions accordingly ensued on two fronts. The LEA and the diocese, aided by the National Society, talked about how to preserve the inclusive Church of England ethos of St Alban's if it became an academy. Meanwhile the head teacher and chair of governors joined a steering group under LEA leadership with their counterparts in six other Birmingham secondary schools to discuss the implications and timetable of becoming academies with new buildings. Because Highgate with its surroundings was the only part of the city where the population was expected to grow, St Alban's was the only prospective academy whose building would allow for increased enrolment. That sounded encouraging.

But the leadership of the city reacted with ambivalence to the prospect of academies. The initiative for their creation came from the schools minister in the Department for Education and Skills (DfES). Academies were to be funded directly by DfES rather than through the LEA as a present. And while the city wanted the accompanying BSF funding from central government for new buildings, it did not want to lose control of the city's schools. That uneasiness was shared by some head teachers, governors and staff in the prospective academies; but it was not much felt at St Alban's because its long-term survival was at stake. The city wanted to retain some control over potential academies through substantial representation on their governing bodies and through local sponsorship. But Andrew Adonis wanted to take the management of failing comprehensive schools away from the Local Education Authorities which had tolerated their poor performance and place it in more ambitious hands in the individual schools. In place of the LEA, every academy would therefore require a sponsor with the skills, resources and power to launch and sustain it on the path to improvement with an endowment of two million pounds. Birmingham's LEA looked to local businesses for this support. The search proved fruitless in Birmingham because industries of the West Midlands worked on much smaller profit margins than the financial interests in the City of London which funded academies there. The political leaders of Birmingham regardless of party, however, had long resented the ability of City finance to override the needs of manufacturing industry upon which the West Midlands depended; and they did not welcome the ability of the schools ministry in London to find sponsorship for Birmingham academies from citadels of City finance. ARK, the educational charity that the schools ministry found for St Alban's, was founded and richly funded by a consortium of hedge funds.

These conflicting instincts and interests prolonged the discussions about forming the first academies in Birmingham. St Alban's found steady support in its quest to become an academy from the diocese under its new Director of Religious Education, Mary Edwards, and from the Trustees of St Alban's School. The negotiating weight of the Trust was enhanced by its ownership of the land on which the existing school stood. But the need for more land to build the expanded new school vexed the discussion because the needed land belonged to three different departments in the city government, each jealously defending its turf.

St Alban's was heartened in the midst of these discussions by an Ofsted inspection, its first since the end of the Octet project, that raised its assessment of the school from satisfactory to good. The inspectors lauded the school for encouraging all students to learn to the best of their ability. 'The headteacher's vision and his very strong direction have resulted in a school where every child mattered and where the inclusive Christian ethos of the school raised its reputation in the local community and attracted students of other faiths.' Ofsted also commended the school for working well in partnership with other educational institutions, all of them aimed at improving students' attainment, personal development and well-being. There were of course aspects of the work of the school that needed improvement, including most seriously underperformance in teaching. But the crucial weakness that the school had always to contend with lay in the exceptionally low attainment of its students on entry at age 11. Three quarters of the entering students had a reading age of eight-year-olds, and only one in ten had a reading age that matched their chronological age. That was the weakness to which David Gould drew cautionary attention when the Ofsted assessment of the school as good was followed by the National Society Statutory Inspection of Anglican Schools assessment of St Alban's as outstanding. The National Society inspector turned St Alban's into a model of the contribution that a Christian school could make to the character and cohesion of a mixed faith and race community.

Ironically, these glowing assessments of the school made its transformation into an academy more difficult. The campaign to create academies was targeted initially at failing schools; and while St Alban's faced exceptionally challenging circumstances, Ofsted inspectors declared that it was meeting those challenges well. That made it an anomalous school for ARK to sponsor, for all the schools that it had hitherto taken on were failing. ARK was reluctant to recognise that St Alban's did not fall into this category. This reluctance stemmed from ARK's insistence on a higher standard for school assessment than that in the Octet project. That project worked on the assumption that the poverty and associated forms of deprivation in its participating schools would prevent many of their students from reaching high levels of academic attainment. The Local Authority and the diocese of Birmingham shared that assumption. But ARK flatly rejected it – as did Andrew Adonis in the schools ministry. ARK also ignored the league table of value added by schools in their teaching and learning, the table in which St Alban's always fared better than in the league tables on straightforward KS3 and GCSE results.

After protracted discussions involving the head teacher and chair of governors, the Diocesan Board of Education, the Local Authority and ARK, agreement was finally reached on turning St Alban's as a Church of England school into an ARK academy. But uneasiness and misunderstanding persisted in many quarters. The diocese was sorry to lose the control that the voluntary aided status of the school had vested in the church. The spokesman for ARK who addressed the Diocesan Board of Education increased its consternation by insisting that, though all legal governing power over ARK academies was vested in the ARK central board, the Local Governing Body (LGB) for St Alban's could not contain more than one representative of the diocese. Yet it was respect for the inclusive Church of England religious ethos of the school that counteracted uneasiness at the Birmingham Central Mosque about the secularism of ARK. There was also dismay at the LEA because it too would be allowed only one representation on the LGB. David Gould applied successfully for appointment as principal of St Alban's as it became an academy. But here again the appointment was anomalous because ARK had consistently replaced the head teachers of the failing schools it had previously taken over. David Gould's collegial style of leadership was also unfamiliar to ARK, which concentrated all its hopes for the transformation of its schools on the principal.

Boys at St Alban's Academy in their smart new uniforms.

The arrangements that were made to turn David Gould from head teacher into principal of the academy accentuated the transformation that was expected in the school: it was to be a step-change. From January to August 2009 St Alban's was placed entirely in the able hands of its deputy head teacher, Sue Walton. David Gould spent that spring term at ARK headquarters in London visiting ARK academies that were already up and running, imbibing their underlying philosophy and observing their practice. Back in Birmingham for the summer term, he was based in a city-centre office rather than at the school, which remained under Sue Walton. But he had ready access to the school to discuss with staff, students and parents all the changes he proposed to make in the

5. Extending Faith in the Inner City

school day, curriculum, teaching and learning practices and student behaviour. These proposals were meanwhile fine tuned in discussions at the headquarters of ARK in London involving its executive director and director of education together with David Gould and the chair of governors of the school who was to remain chair of a reconstructed Local Governing Body for the academy.

The discussions in London proved more strenuous than those in Birmingham. Despite opposition from the teachers unions, most of the teachers and non-teaching staff were willing to try out the longer school day that David Gould proposed in order to increase teaching time, particularly for literacy. Their terms and conditions of employment could remain the same, and though the school day would be longer, the number of student contact hours for teachers would remain unchanged. Students responded with pleasure to the handsome blue trimmed uniforms they were to wear; David Gould prepared them for the strict behavioural code that the academy would enforce; and the parents welcomed it. But that code was tougher than David Gould initially desired because student behaviour at St Alban's was already better than in surrounding schools and was frequently praised. It was, however, not good enough to meet ARK's insistence that no teaching time in the classroom be lost because of unruly students. Henceforth any student who required a second warning about misbehaviour would be detained in school at the end of the day and, if repeatedly unruly, brought back on Saturday morning.

There was a palpable sense of step-change with the formal closure of the school at the end of August and opening of St Alban's Academy at the beginning of September 2009. It was reflected in the school uniform, not jumpers any longer but blazers as in high aspiring schools, and by the look of anticipation on the faces of the children. But the changes in teaching methodology aroused uneasiness among the teachers, and some of them were slow to grasp the need for detailed assessment data on the progress and objectives for each student. Though the final set of GCSE results for the school showed marked improvement, the level of achievement, particularly in English, remained worrying. ARK set high targets for student achievement and took no account of socio-economic background. As for behaviour, one third of the students found themselves in detention at the end of the day, and the number was slow to fall. It produced one pleasant surprise: the previously most unruly students accepted the new regime readily because they no longer felt singled out unfairly. And a still greater benefit gradually became apparent. The amount of stress-related illness and absence among the staff began to fall as they encountered less difficulty bringing their students into line.

The first year in the adjustment to the new regime proved strenuous and sometimes disappointing. The city authorities moved sluggishly in commissioning the new building that St Alban's was to receive under the BSF programme, the date for its completion slipped from 2012 to 2013, and it fell deeper into question with word that the new Coalition government at Westminster might bring the BSF programme to a halt. Uncertainty in Highgate about what the change into an academy meant for St Alban's contributed to a fall in admissions expected for the coming school year. The city moved the centre of the Highgate Education Action Zone, which had cultivated good relations with surrounding feeder primary schools, away from St Alban's because it was no longer under city control.

Even so, all would be well if the academy clearly improved the performance of its students in the all-important GCSE results. The academy targeted attention on the Year 11 students who would take their GCSEs in June, and gave individual tuition to those on the borderline between D and C in English and mathematics. The timetable was revised throughout the school to provide additional teaching in English and mathematics. The curriculum was also revised in line with the ARK policy of depth before breadth, paying more attention to English and mathematics before worrying about the broader requirements of the national curriculum. Using data gathered from the autumn term reports, target-setting days were established when the students accompanied by their parents would come to the school to discuss their individual goals subject by subject. One dividend of this approach was increased involvement of parents in the education of their children, a dividend with wide-ranging rewards.

Other ways to improve teaching and learning were developed as the year advanced. One of the most valuable but also most testing was frequent observation and assessment of classroom teaching by the Senior Leadership Team and less frequent but more rigorous monitoring visits by the Director of Education at ARK, Sir Michael Wilshaw. While the SLT concentrated initially on newly qualified and recent university graduate Teach First teachers, Sir Michael and his colleagues looked in on classes throughout the school. Another innovation was the establishment of an Academy learning team led by one of the best teachers at the school with assistance from ARK central staff to improve the quality and consistency of teaching across the curriculum and share best practice among the teaching staff. Training programmes were introduced to help struggling teachers. Still the monitoring visits drew relentless attention to how far teaching and learning at St Alban's needed to improve. The mood in the school at the end of its first year as an academy was sombre.

But it erupted in delight when the GCSE results in August 2010 exceeded the school's highest hopes. ARK had prevailed upon the school to aim for 42 per cent 5 A*-Cs, this time including English and mathematics, well above the 31 per cent achieved in the previous year and more than many thought likely. Staff and students alike were staggered that 50 per cent of those who took GCSEs that June had secured 5 grades of A*-C including English and mathematics, the highest increase in any ARK school in its first year as an academy. These results upheld ARK's faith that examination results of children in the most deprived neighbourhoods in the country could rise as rapidly as those in privileged districts. The results also convinced the staff that the stiff pace of improvement in teaching set by ARK really worked. The GCSE results that St Alban's attained that August were a triumph for the teachers as much as for the students.

The school received further encouragement from the news that planning for its new building could go ahead. Enrolment in September also rose to 442, and the annual turnover of students caused by endless movement of families in and out of Highgate, which made it hard to sustain improvement, declined. Still, the GCSE results at St Alban's were on the whole no better than the national average. There was a long way to go before the school reached and sustained proven excellence. The immediate challenge was to extend the successful preparation for the GCSEs at the end of Key Stage 4 to beginning students in Key Stage 3. The greatest threat to achievement at St Alban's invariably stemmed from the extremely low attainment of its students on entry. Another challenge lay at the end of Key Stage 4 where grades of A*-C would not be enough to qualify students for entry into the Sixth Form which St Alban's was to set up once the new building opened. For that the students would need A*-Bs.

St Alban's was both heartened and challenged that autumn by a preliminary visit from Ofsted to prepare the school for its definitive inspection the following year. Like the Octet project, this preliminary report began by recognising the immensity of the challenges amidst which St Alban's worked, with levels of economic deprivation and ethnic diversity far above the national average and levels of student attainment on entry far below. It praised the school's GCSE success and the quality of teaching particularly in mathematics and engineering. Attainment in English was still well below average but improving rapidly. The inspectors were also impressed by the calm and respectful behaviour of the students. Ofsted nonetheless endorsed the core principle of ARK that students in the most deprived corners of the country could reach levels of academic attainment as high as more privileged students. The Ofsted inspectors pointed out that there were still pockets of poor performance at St Alban's and under achievement in some major subjects. Overall, while the inspectors found good progress towards raising attainment, they urged the school to accelerate the improvement in teaching and learning particularly in the daily literacy time and called for better use of assessment information and more consistency in marking.

The school took this guidance to heart and addressed the shortcomings that this preliminary Ofsted report identified while extending across the school the approaches to teaching and learning that had produced the wonderful GCSE results of August. The academic as distinct from vocational components of the curriculum were strengthened to prepare students for sixth form work and also for the requirements of the new English Baccalaureate which placed renewed emphasis on the humanities, individual sciences and foreign languages. For the same purposes, the longer school day already in effect for Key Stage 3 was extended to Key Stage 4, a development that both students and parents welcomed. The response of the surrounding community to the school's first year as an academy was reflected in rising applications for entry to the school, and it found itself oversubscribed. Monitoring inspections by the Director of Education at ARK drew attention to the need for closer, more individually tailored teaching of entering students with the lowest levels of literacy, and an outstanding specialist was recruited to address this need.

Always and on every front the school focused its attention on improving the standard of teaching and learning. Throughout the school the pace of teaching quickened, accurate data was assembled on the rate of achievement of each student and individual goals were set for them in each subject, escalating goals with which students as well as teachers became familiar. Teachers and students learned to expect more of each other. Middle management was strengthened for Key Stage 3, particularly in English. As for Key Stage 4, stretching to the upper limits of what he thought attainable, the principal strove to ensure that, at the end of the school's second year as an academy, 55 per cent of the students taking GCSEs would achieve A*-C grades in at least 5 subjects including English and mathematics. Students and staff alike held their breath at the end of the summer term of 2011 to see if they reached this goal.

They were staggered, almost incredulous to find that not 55 but 67 per cent had done so, more than double the 31 per cent in the school's last year before becoming an academy. But even that success did not quite prepare the school for the judgement delivered by Ofsted two months later. Let its inspectors speak for themselves: 'St Alban's Academy gives richness and meaning to many students' lives and provides an outstanding standard of education. The Principal provides the key inspiration for the overall success of the academy. ... he is also able to develop high standards of leadership in others. ... There is a clear vision that all can succeed. This aim is central to the academy, where learning is the way of life. Staff and students alike work hard, display an ambition to succeed and a commitment to do their best ... rooted in the belief that all students should have access to high-quality learning experiences. Consequently, from exceptionally low attainment on entry, students leave with above average attainment and outstanding achievement.' The inspectors praised the teaching at the school as consistently good and very often outstanding.

Also outstanding was the 'spiritual, moral, social and cultural development that underpins students' exemplary behaviour and makes an exceptional contribution to their excellent learning.' The religious faith of the founders of the school had combined with the educational faith of ARK in the learning capacity of inner-city students to produce an academy which the prime minister promptly singled out for praise. The National Society inspector who came after Ofsted reinforced this assessment, praising St Alban's as a model of service by a Church of England school in a religiously diverse community: 'St Alban's Academy successfully encourages students to live by faith, developing mutual respect and thus forming a bridge between cultures. Within this ethos, a relentless drive for success ensures that academic as well as personal progress is outstanding.' That ethos was consolidated by the appointment in the autumn term of a chaplain from Pakistan to strengthen the interfaith ministry of the school.

The main area for improvement that the Ofsted inspectors challenged the school to address lay in the low proportion of A*-A grades in its otherwise impressive GCSE results. This challenge led directly to the next step in the school's quest for excellence, opening the sixth form for which the new building was designed. Students who did not secure higher grade As and Bs in the subjects they wanted to pursue in sixth form would not be able to meet its demands. Rather that delay opening the sixth form until the students were ready for it, the principal turned the challenge around. He selected the leadership and marshalled the teaching staff for the sixth form and prepared the students in the earlier years of Key Stage 3 and 4 to handle the work at that level as soon as the new building would allow. The eagerness of the parents for early access to the sixth form for their children encouraged the principal to take this step. The response of the community to the rising achievement of the school was further reflected when, for the first time since the nineteenth century, the school found itself oversubscribed by first choice applicants for admission.

The hitherto unceasing pace of improvement at the school was checked in August 2012 by a fall in the GCSE results in English and hence in the percentage of students receiving A*-C grades in five subjects including English and mathematics, down from the level achieved in the previous year and well below target. There were several reasons for the shortfall in the English results including a change in the syllabus, in the form of assessment, and in the grading between January and June. The school learned what it could from the setback, encouraged by the improvement in its GCSE results in most other subjects including science, previously an area of weakness, and in Key Stage 3. The relentless pace of improvement in the early and intermediate years at the school bode well for the future.

St Alban's is emerging as one of the jewels in Birmingham's secondary school crown. It has been singled out by the Specialist Schools and Academy Trust as 'one of the best schools in the country at outperforming expectations for their pupils and improving their future prospects.' The *Financial Times* has lauded it as 'an Anglican secondary school that is performing miracles in a Muslim neighbourhood where one in three working-age adults are either unable to work or cannot find jobs.' Becoming an ARK academy has given St Alban's more than its leaders initially looked for and has amplified the faith that it was founded to serve. St Alban's has in turn proved rewarding for ARK and is a pace setter and model of good practice in the ARK network, now expanding in Birmingham as well as London. As we move into our new building and open our sixth form, we enter upon another step-change in our advancing faith in the inner city.